HOW TO GET THE MOST OUT OF THIS COURSE

SUGGESTIONS FOR GROUP MEMBERS

1. THE MATERIAL Scattered through the text are boxes containing a variety of quotes. They do not necessarily refer directly to that page – or even that session. They're there to trigger some thoughts. You can ignore them completely if you like – though some people say that they're one of the best bits!

2. PREPARATION It'll help you enormously if you're able to have your own personal copy of this booklet (so the price is reduced either when multiple copies are ordered or if you order online). Try to have read each session *before* the meeting.

3. USING A TRANSCRIPT The Transcript booklet is a c———'— record of the words as spoken on the audio material. It may help you to feel _____ give you greater confidence about joining in the disc_ leisure after the session may help you absorb the text

SUGGESTIONS FOR GROUP LEADERS

We're deliberately not prescriptive, and different lead__ ┌__ different ways, but here are a few tried and trusted ideas …

1. THE ROOM Discourage people from sitting outside or behind the main circle – it's good for all to feel equally involved.

2. HOSPITALITY Tea or coffee and biscuits on arrival and/or at the end of a meeting is always appreciated and encourages people to talk informally.

3. THE START If group members don't know each other well, some kind of 'icebreaker' might be helpful. For example, you might invite people to share something about themselves and/or about their faith. Be careful to place a time limit on this exercise!

4. PREPARING THE GROUP Explain that there are no right or wrong answers, and that among friends it is fine to say things that you are not sure about – to express half-formed ideas. If individuals choose to say nothing, that is all right too.

5. THE MATERIAL Encourage members to read each session *before* the meeting. It helps if each group member has their own personal copy of this booklet. **There is no need to consider all the questions.** A lively exchange of views is what matters, so be selective.

6. PREPARATION Decide beforehand whether to distribute (or ask people to bring) paper, pencils, hymn books etc. If you're going to ask anyone to do anything e.g. lead prayer or read a Bible passage, do give them advance notice so they can prepare.

7. TIMING Try to start on time and make sure you stick fairly closely to your stated finishing time.

8. USING THE AUDIO MATERIAL The track markers on the audio (and shown in the Transcript) will help you find your way around the recorded material very easily. For each of the sessions we recommend reading through the session in the course booklet, before listening together to all of the relevant session on the audio. And then tackle the Questions for Groups.

9. USING THE TRANSCRIPT The Transcript is a complete record of the words as spoken on the audio material. You'll find this invaluable as you prepare. Group members will undoubtedly benefit from having a copy, if they so wish.

INTRODUCTION
So what are you waiting for?

This course is all about time and our attitude towards it. In the four weeks before Christmas we wait for the coming of Christ from eternity into time, and the traditional way the Church has celebrated the season of Advent is by meditating on what are known as the 'Four Last Things': Death, Judgement, Heaven and Hell.

Advent isn't simply a time of waiting for Christmas, but has a sense of apocalypse about it - waiting not only for Jesus to be born in Bethlehem, but waiting for Jesus to come at the end of time. Sunday readings during Advent are fierce: we read the prophets and their lacerating criticism of an unjust world. We read the gospel insistence that time is short. We read about wise virgins trimming their lamps, about the labour pangs of the universe, about the harsh master condemning the unforgiving slave to a place where there is wailing and gnashing of teeth. Advent is a season when the concerns of the Church seem very far from the tinsel-strewn shopping centres that make up December in the secular world.

And underlying much of the Church's meditation on the end times, on the urgency of Jesus's message and the attentive waiting of the prophets is a meditation on time itself. It's an obvious thing to say, but we can't avoid living in time, which, as we sometimes say, marches on. Our language is peppered with phrases about time: we talk about killing time, wasting time, spending time, making up time – as if it were a commodity, something we could see and touch. But we know we can't and the truth is that much of our experience of living in time depends on our state of mind and heart, and our life circumstances, not to mention our age.

Although it's a particular theme for Advent, the fact that the gospels are full of Jesus's sayings about time and how short it is means that these are themes that can be explored at any time of the year. The beauty of the liturgical seasons is that we know that while we celebrate one at a time, all are present at once. We are Easter people - always living this side of the resurrection - but we are always also Advent people: expectant, waiting, listening for prophecies and deepening our hope.

So, spending four sessions looking together at the Bible's guidance, contemplating our own spiritual lives, and exploring some of the theology that arises from that will be, as they say, time well spent.

'Go with haste'

Read: Luke 2.8-20

The title of this first session is taken from Luke's account in the second chapter of his gospel, of the shepherds hurrying to Bethlehem after the amazing experience they have of a vision of angels. Their ordinary night shift in the fields has been interrupted by this experience that they can't explain. We're told in Luke's gospel that they are terrified, but that after they have taken in the enormity of what they are experiencing, they 'went with haste' to find the child.

It's a cliché to say it (but then clichés are often painfully true) that in the 21st century we are living life in too much of a hurry. The astonishing pace of change, most especially in the immediate access to information on the internet, means that we are living quickly. Perhaps too quickly for us to cope with. I've noticed that day-to-day conversations which used to be punctuated by comments such as, 'now, what was his name?' or 'there's a great book I'm reading but I can't remember who by' or 'do you know the way to the post office?' are

> "To every thing there is a season and a time to every purpose under heaven"
>
> *Ecclesiastes Chapter 3*

often now interrupted by a couple of seconds on a smartphone and the information has been retrieved. No one ever need worry about forgetting the name of the TV programme they liked; we just Google it.

This is, of course, fantastic - something our ancestors could never have dreamed was possible. The World Wide Web and its democratic processes mean that people can be contacted, facts can be corrected, and all manner of problems solved with an entry into an internet browser. But it does also mean that the pace of activity is ever quicker. There's less time to consider things, less need to mull things over.

And there seems, more seriously, less opportunity to wonder about things, to meander through the thoughts we might have, when we can always bring our musings to a halt by simply looking stuff up. And alongside the beneficial consequences, some of the effects aren't so good. One evolutionary biologist has identified the mismatch between our brains, which are essentially still the same as they were in the Stone Age, and modern technologically-driven life, as a basis for the diagnosis of depression. We are just not yet hard-wired to flourish in an environment where mostly we are not in physical survival mode. The proliferation of information, the speed of decision making, the sheer volume of contact and communication which is open to us challenges our brains profoundly and can cause a greater sense of panic, anxiety and emotional disorder than we are usually willing to admit.

Good haste and bad haste

Actually, I want to suggest that there is good haste and bad haste. Mostly we use it in a negative way as in the phrase 'More haste, less speed' where you rush to put your shoes on and fall over in the process. This kind of haste implies an unseemly hurry. It implies that you haven't really thought it through, that you're over-busy. There will be times in all our lives when we feel we simply don't have a moment to ourselves, and can't remember the last time we had time to take stock or think something through, let alone actually pray.

But it's true too that a fast-paced life full of commitments, personal or professional, can feel exhilarating. The catchphrase used by the fictional President Bartlett in the TV drama series *West Wing* was: 'What's next?' Even immediately after some international crisis in the situation room, when troops had had to be deployed and war had been once again averted at the last minute, he would turn to his Chief of Staff and say, 'What's next?' This kind of 'what's next?' life can be a life lived as if on tiptoe; expectant; curious. It doesn't have to be a hasty life; it can be simply a full and varied life.

The truth is that only we know the quality of the time we live, and whether our busy-ness is healthy or draining. We know too that a habit of haste can be, whatever our activity level, a way of hiding ourselves away. You know the kind of thing: in conversation, I might talk too much because I'm actually a bit afraid of what might happen if I stopped. If I let a silence fall, someone might ask me how I am - and I might just tell them. So to avoid this, I will let my stories tumble over themselves and my words will fill the space. Phew! Got away with it again.

Making sure we are keeping busy is one way that people deal with grief. Fair enough. But not forever. Hasty living is an easily acquired habit and is not dependent on what we are actually doing. A retired widow living alone can be living a more internally hasty life than the President of the United States if she is afraid of what might happen if she doesn't have a mind full of distraction. A life lived in haste will form over time an effective mask that will hide our long-held sorrows, suppressed fears, and sometimes, quiet despair.

> "Most men pursue pleasure with such breathless haste that they hurry past it."
>
> *Søren Kierkegaard, Danish Philosopher*

> "I'm far too busy not to pray for two hours a day."
>
> *Archbishop Desmond Tutu*

A hurry habit can be the curse of an anxious work place too, where in an attempt to drive up either standards or profit, or both, what could be an exhilarating and productive atmosphere becomes one where employees feel that whatever they do, it's simply never enough. Dissatisfaction reigns.

Is hurry a form of greed?

It could also be that our tendency to hurry is a form of greed. Greed for time itself. We are focussed on saving time (although for what, we often don't quite know) and so gobbling up experiences, making sure we're moving on, not lingering or wondering or musing, can again become a habit that's hard to break. We gulp and don't sip; we shove it in instead of folding it up; we shoot the red light instead of slowing down as we approach; we make sure time is never wasted and we are irritated when we think it is. We say, 'mustn't stop', we 'get it done' so that 'it's over with'.

Before long, we realise that from the moment we wake up to the moment we finally go to bed (making sure we're very tired before we do, so that we don't lie awake too much) we are hurrying through the day. Every day. Even - perhaps especially - when there's not much to do.

So maybe sometimes our habit of haste is us being greedy – and we can find that our eyes really were bigger than our stomach. A hasty life can become a bloated life; over full of quick fix information but craving the more satisfying wisdom.

Finding wisdom

Wisdom can be found in Luke's story of Biblical haste by an ordinary group of men at work, and their choices about what made them hurry and what made them stop. Maybe we can see in the shepherds' story that good haste is creative, responsive and brings us joy.

In the shepherds' case, their lives were turned upside-down in an instant by very strange happenings on what they assumed would be an ordinary night. Suddenly they were energised, and their rushing to the town to find Jesus was partly as a result of their being 'terrified'.

As soon as the vision of angels had gone, they said, 'let us go now'. No more waiting. Their priority was suddenly and dramatically clear, and they took action immediately with no delay. There had been some kind of rush of adrenaline linked with their fear that got them up off the ground, making a journey that moments earlier they wouldn't have dreamed of making. Their response was creative, energetic, wanting to see for themselves and – importantly - now.

Sometimes, when things are important, really important, going now with haste is absolutely the right thing to do. These shepherds were, for God's sake, eyewitnesses to the story of salvation unfolding before them. They didn't wait to hear about it from someone else. They disrupted their normal pattern of work and life; they left their usual surroundings and just went.

One night in August

I remember an evening in August 1991. I was on holiday in the West Country with members of the L'Arche community in which I was living at the time. We heard on the news that the journalist John McCarthy was going to be released after five years in captivity. He had been held by the group Islamic Jihad and for some reason, his story, and the efforts of his family and friends to keep him in the news, had struck a chord with me ever since his capture in 1986. I realised that RAF Lyneham was only a couple of hours away and, on the spur of

the moment, I jumped into the car with one of our L'Arche members. We took sandwiches and a flask and went to see what we could see. In the event, we were part of a small crowd that gathered and waited for a long time by the wire perimeter fence until it was dark.

When the plane came into view, we were choked; we hugged strangers as it landed, and a few moments later we could just make out a shadowy figure walking out of the plane. We cheered just in case he could hear us. There was nothing to see really, but my companion and I were elated. We had been there. We witnessed with our own eyes something we, along with the rest of the country, never thought we'd see. And despite the four-hour round trip, the waiting, and the fact we couldn't see much at all, I am proud even to this day to say that I was there.

Just Do It

Good haste can spur us on and face down the nay-saying voices that might stop us from taking a risk or a punt. The sentiment behind the 'let's go' that the shepherds said is repeated in numerous sayings - probably most memorably in modern times by the advertising slogan for the sports firm Nike: 'Just do it'.

Perhaps the nub of the question then is not tackling a hurry habit by just deciding to sit down or, as Pope Francis scolded young people at a youth mass in Krakov in 2016, by becoming a 'couch potato'. It is not about becoming quietist in the face of all the challenges that life brings personally, socially, ethically. But it is asking ourselves a version of John the Baptist's question to the crowd who had travelled out to him in the desert: 'What did you come out to see?' If we have a sense of the priorities we want to live by, then there will be times when we move quickly, decisively, take a risk and, by acting in faith, deepen our experience of God in the world. By contrast, if we become enthralled to

> "Haste is of the Devil."
>
> *St Jerome*

hasty living because it helps us to avoid the fundamental truths of our lives, then our spiritual challenge is to both slow down and summon up all our courage to face what it is we are avoiding. And, like the shepherds, spend our energy in turning and returning to God and God alone.

Questions for Groups

1. Are you a 'hurrier 'or a 'time-taker'? Are you happy about this? *Track 2 of the audio/transcript.*

2. Are you a risk-taker? What is worth taking a risk for? What in your life are you prepared to risk? Is anything a risk if you have Christ in your life and on your side?

3. Do you recognise the distinction between good haste and bad haste? Tell a story from your own life that might illustrate either.

4. How do you feel about the internet? Do you feel it's a blessing or a curse? *Track 6 of the audio/transcript.*

5. The shepherds made haste to the stable because it was obviously important for them to do so. Do you find it easy or difficult to distinguish between what's urgent and what's important?

6. Do you commit time to saying prayers or reading the Bible? Why do you think many of us find making time for this so hard? *Track 8 of the audio/transcript.*

7. In the Christian tradition, greed or avarice is one of the seven deadly sins. Do you agree with Lucy's idea that hurry and haste can themselves be a form of greed? *See p.5.*

8. Just do it! Or wait and it will become clear what you should do. Which camp do you fall into? *See p.6 and track 10.*

'How Long O Lord how long?'

Read: Psalm 13

The Scriptures that Jesus knew were the Jewish Scriptures of the prophets and the psalms. This session's title comes from one of the 150 psalms that made up a kind of hymn book for worship in the Temple. Each psalm is a song that helped all those who heard it or sang it themselves to tell the story of God's people: their trials and battles, their triumphs and their failures. Psalm 13 begins with the phrase *'How long O Lord? Will you forget me forever? How long will you hide your face from me?'*

And the author knew what he was talking about. King David, said to be the writer of this psalm, led what could be called a colourful life, full of family intrigue, battles against his rivals, a rather chaotic private life and - the greatest tragedy of his life - the violent death of his son Absalom. This then is a cry born of life experience, a cry of dereliction, a sense that God is hiding from him – that he can't see where God is in his life. This is the kind of thing thought about and prayed about by people all over the world of every faith and language.

The psalms themselves are a fantastic source of honest, sometimes bracing, challenging cries to God. They can be shocking: challenging God profoundly about personal circumstances or blaming God, or desperately asking God to destroy the people who are 'enemies'. And the cry that we are considering this session: *How long O Lord?* is one that has been powerful for generations of people stuck in a situation they don't want or can't tolerate.

'How long?' is a question alive today in refugee camps around the world, in housing estates overrun by gangs, in villages waiting for rain, and in the quiet despair of domestic abuse.

Waiting for things to change. Waiting for life to get better. Waiting for circumstances to improve - for the boss to resign or the child to come back or the night to fall. Waiting takes many forms, both profound and mundane. We all do it, mostly we try to reduce it, and some of us even say we hate it. Waiting is something that often evokes emotion in us, frustration or fury in equal measure.

> "Patience is a virtue, possess it if you can -
> seldom found in woman, and never in a man."
>
> *Attributed to philosopher John Dewey*

Waiting and status

In our society, people who wait are usually people who are poor. Eliminating waiting is a sign of status or wealth.

Instead of waiting for the bus home, he orders a car to be waiting for him after the meeting. Instead of waiting for a slot to come up with the GP, she sees a doctor within 24 hours under her private insurance. The one who waits is lower status than the one who doesn't have to.

This reveals a fundamental reflection about time in a modern mechanised and complex society. For systems to work well, there often needs to be a physical space where those in the system can wait. It keeps things running on time; it keeps things efficient. A highly skilled person like a doctor needs to be made the most of, and so her day is parcelled up into 10-minute appointments. So as not to waste her time, there is a place for people to wait to see her. She doesn't wait. But they do. It is a sign that her time is more highly valued by society. And we move between these roles all the time. That same GP could visit her bank at lunchtime, and have to stand in line until a cashier is free.

By the same token, keeping someone waiting is often used as a way to dominate or intimidate. It's a tool used sometimes to do just that because it demands a different level of knowledge from both parties. The one who waits doesn't have

> "Change will not come if we wait for some other person or some other time. We are the ones we've been waiting for. We are the change that we seek."
>
> *Barack Obama*

any idea (usually) how long this is going to last. The one who keeps the other waiting is in control, not only of the agenda and order of things, but seemingly of time itself. It can change the dynamic of a meeting.

Time waits for no one

There are some more fundamental ways in which we all wait. For a flower to bloom; for a baby to arrive; for a loved one to die.

But as the 12th century English poet Geoffrey Chaucer noted in the Clerk's Tale from the famous Canterbury Tales: 'For though we sleep, or wake or roam, or ride, time flies and waits for no one'. In other words, whether we're active or not, busy or still, time will continue to pass. It waits for no one.

In W H Vanstone's famous book *The Stature of Waiting,* waiting is one of the key aspects attributed to Jesus's life and ministry precisely because it is a low status activity. Christian waiting is a challenge to a world that says the only valuable life is a productive life. Waiting in an attentive way, in an alert way, will mean that you become more aware of the world and its rhythms; you notice more of how and who people are, not just what they are achieving.

I am in the middle of what they call 'working age' - in my 40s and, like many people, working pretty hard. But I have, over time, modified my attitude towards time and how I view it. I remember some years ago talking to a friend who said that he had turned up to catch a train, but he hadn't looked up the precise time. He knew they went about every 15 minutes so there would be one soon whatever time he arrived. At the time, I was feeling under a lot of pressure at work, and I remember being totally bemused that he could live like this. My day was parcelled up into slots of, I realised at the time, 15 minutes. Every single slot was allocated. And I didn't have any to spare. Certainly none to spare standing around on a draughty station platform. Not only this, but actually the truth is, I judged him. I thought unfairly and secretly that his time was obviously not as precious as mine. This conversation stayed with me and I noticed in an instant that things had got out of hand. We spoke about it at the time, and have laughed about it ever since.

Like many priests, a good chunk of my work time is spent with people who are not at work. Meetings in the evening or at weekends, Sunday services, parish away-days or lunchtime eucharists for local workers. My work time is other people's off time - time that they generously give to our church

> "Patience is power.
> Patience is not an absence of action;
> rather it is "timing"
> it waits on the right time to act,
> for the right principles
> and in the right way."
>
> *Archbishop Fulton J Sheen*

community. But because of the parish I'm currently in, I'm also working with people at work. Because we employ over 20 people much of my time is spent in line management, planning, budgeting and all the day-to-day dynamics of paid employment.

Attitudes to Waiting

In each environment, I detect a different attitude to waiting. And we often talk about trying to eliminate the difference. I wonder what it is about 'work time' that makes it somehow feel really different from 'time off'; and how that affects our attitude to waiting. I spend quite a bit of my time with people who are older than me – who describe themselves as 'retired'. I enjoy it. But there is one aspect to 'retirement', speaking as someone who isn't there yet, that I do wonder about. I often hear retired people saying how busy they are. And sometimes they say it in even more urgent a way than people who are still at work. I think there is something in there about status and anxiety that other people won't think they are living as productive a life if they don't fill their time. People often say things like, 'I don't know how I ever had time to have a job'. Being active and fulfilled is obviously fantastic for as long as possible. But I do love it when retired people don't say things like that, because I think that within a church community of people of all ages, older people with different priorities and a sense of perspective about time are a gift to the rest of us. And I wish sometimes they could teach me my mistakes about status by not wanting to be busy all the time.

The stature of waiting

I suppose the distinction I'm trying to get at is that we sometimes mistake activity for purpose. And we sometimes mistake inactivity for waste. And there are insights here, not just for living a healthy life, but for life lived consonant with the purposes and will of God. In W H Vanstone's book, he identifies a significant shift in the gospel story from the three years or so spent by Jesus healing, travelling, preaching in the hills of Galilee, the city of Capernaum and the temple in Jerusalem; a shift from these three active years to the pivotal moment in the garden of Gethsemane when Jesus is 'handed over' by Judas to the political establishment. From this

> "Each life is made up of mistakes and learning, waiting and growing, practising patience and being persistent."
> *Billy Graham*

moment, Jesus moves from active to passive, literally suffering in his passion what is done to him by a frightened, competitive and violent humanity, intent on maintaining its political power and religious status quo. From Gethsemane onwards, Jesus is made to wait. And it is at that moment that he chooses to be made to wait. In him, God waits on the vagaries of politicians and the fickleness of a crowd.

We believe that God is omnipotent, but in Jesus, God became subject to human authority. God was made to wait, made to be passive. When human beings do this to each other, it is normally out of fear and a desire to dominate each other. But Jesus freely chose to become passive. He allowed it to happen to him, and by becoming undefended in the face of human violence the world was saved. Human domination can never finally win again. In the story of Jesus's mock trial and crucifixion, he teaches us what God is like but more challengingly perhaps teaches what human life could be like too: it is life lived attentively, expectant of a new future. And in the light of the resurrection, we can know too that no one else's violence will ultimately destroy us.

> "Are you ready?" Klaus asked finally.
> "No," Sunny answered.
> "Me neither," Violet said, "but if we wait until we're ready we'll be waiting for the rest of our lives, Let's go."
> *Lemony Snicket: 'The Ersatz Elevator'*

Restlessness

It does also seem part of the Christian vocation to live with a degree of yearning and restlessness too. It is sometimes called living in the 'Now and the Not Yet': reaching towards something more than this; longing for a better world, a deeper justice, a brighter hope. And one of the more challenging aspects of this yearning is that we learn to acknowledge it at all and don't bury it. As we go on through life, it's usually easier not to keep yearning for something better. If our expectations are low, then we won't be disappointed.

Over the years, writers on Christian spirituality have been divided on the place of this kind of yearning or desire in spiritual matters. For some, our yearnings are suspect, can't be trusted and should be resisted. For others, such as St Ignatius of Loyola, the founder of the Jesuits, our yearnings are material for spiritual reflection; they are to be examined, accepted and incorporated into our spiritual lives. But it's not always easy to know what our deepest yearnings are. It's sometimes been said that one of the hardest questions to answer truthfully is 'what do you want?' But for us to discover what our deepest yearnings truly are, we have to somehow agree to let them be what they actually are, not what we think they are.

Bartimaeus

One of the most vivid examples of this is in Jesus's encounter with Bartimaeus (Mark 10.46-52). Bartimaeus is by the roadside. Because he is blind, he's relying on listening to the sounds of the crowd, and so when he hears the commotion, he speaks up, trying to get Jesus's attention. Jesus's reply is really surprising in the sense that he simply asks an open question of this man who is blind: 'What is it you want me to do for you?'

I have always been very moved that Jesus doesn't just assume that Bartimaeus wants to be able to see. He could have asked for money, or for help finding a wife, or for a job – anything. Jesus looked at this man and saw him as a whole person, not just a person with an obvious need, and simply asked him to say what it was that he wanted. As it happened, Bartimaeus did ask for his sight. But I've often been struck by how differently Jesus acted in that situation from how most of us might act. When we encounter people, we can't help but make an assessment of who they are and what they might need from us. In a church context,

> "We need to find God, and he cannot be found in noise and restlessness. God is the friend of silence. See how nature - trees, flowers, grass- grows in silence; see the stars, the moon and the sun, how they move in silence... We need silence to be able to touch souls."
>
> *Mother Teresa*

where we think we should probably be nice to each other, we can find ourselves making assumptions about each other and what help we might need.

Not long ago I met with a widow who was trying to be gracious about the questions people were asking her about how she was. She was saying that what she actually wanted was some help with the insurance and the utility companies and picking up the children from school. What she was receiving was food and kindly-meant quotations from bereavement books and the Bible. What she needed was to say the same things over and over again, to tell the story of how her husband had died, and for people not to stay too long. What was happening was that some people were staying away altogether, while others seemed more upset than she was, so she ended up comforting them.

We talked about the fact that when kind people offered to do something to help, it wasn't actually help unless she herself defined it as help. People might have thought they were helping, but in her mind, she allowed herself to say that it wasn't actually help unless she said it was. She was trying to claw back some

> "Aside from velcro, time is the most mysterious substance in the universe. You can't see it or touch it, yet a plumber can charge you upwards of 75 dollars per hour for it, without necessarily fixing anything."
>
> *Dave Barry, American author & humorist*

> "We must be willing to let go of the life we have planned, so as to have the life that is waiting for us."
>
> *E M Forster*

measure of control in a situation that had left her out of control and reeling.

An unexamined life?

We don't have to be too hard on ourselves about all this. From the very best of motives, we're often susceptible to believing that we know what other people need, and inadvertently we stop listening to them, or asking them open questions - let alone actually listening to their answers. As C S Lewis drily remarked in his *Screwtape Letters*: 'She was the kind of woman who lived for others. You could tell the Others by their hunted expression.' And we fall into this way of being when we leave our own deepest desires unexamined.

For Ignatius Loyola, it was essential to take our own needs and desires very seriously. And this meant imaginative contemplation of the Scriptures. He believed that underneath all our superficial desires was our deepest desire to be happy, that is, to be at one with God and for our will to be in tune with the will of God. If we could journey ever more deeply into the well of our own experience, the life we have lived and are living, in the light of the gospels, we would come to the underlying deepest desire of all creatures made in the image of God; to be at one with their Creator, and to live the life for which we were created. As the old saying goes, when I get to heaven, God is not going to ask me why I wasn't Mother Theresa or Martin Luther King. God is going to ask me why I wasn't Lucy Winkett.

The Scriptures teach us that our deepest yearnings are part of a greater yearning for wholeness, for healing, for peace. And so we pray, 'How long, O Lord?' knowing that there is no clear answer about when, but that this attentive waiting is the way we are called to live.

Questions for Groups

1. Do you think of yourself as a patient person? What is your own attitude towards waiting and being kept waiting - what emotions do either evoke in you?

2. What do you think of the idea that waiting is linked to status, power and control? Have you ever been made to wait or kept others waiting? What stories do you have to tell?

3. What do you think of the link between us knowing our own needs and desires well and being able to attend to others? How well do you handle the mismatch between what you need and what others are offering you? *See p.13.*

4. The gospels portray Jesus in his last week as a victim of political manoeuvring. W H Vanstone argues that, in this passive waiting period after Jesus is handed over, he makes holy the human experience of being at the mercy of others. Do you agree with this? Do you see Jesus as a passive victim? *Track 15 of the audio/transcript.*

5. Re-read the paragraph about 'Restlessness' on *p.12*. What is the single most important change that you long for to bring about a better world or society? How does your faith support you in your efforts towards this?

6. 'By living in the world I am participating in God's life' says Lucy. Do we have to be able to love ourselves first in order to be able to love others?

7. Does the story of Bartimaeus help you to think about disability in a different way? *See p.12 and tracks 17 & 18 of the audio/transcript.*

8. Lucy writes, 'I want God to somehow reveal to me, open to me, what my life is, and how my life is.' Do you feel you are living the life God wants you to? Do you feel you (ever) see yourself as God sees you? *See final para on p.13 and track 20 of the audio/transcript.*

9. Are there different life circumstances of people in your group - working, retired, bringing up children? How do these circumstances affect your attitude towards waiting?

Be prepared!

Read Matthew 25.1-13

'Be prepared!' comes not from the Bible, but from the book *Scouting for Boys* by Lord Baden Powell, the founder of the Scout movement in England. His love of the outdoors, his military experience and sense of adventure meant that in 1908 he was writing the rules for a new worldwide movement that is experiencing something of a renaissance today. At the time of writing the Chief Scout is TV presenter and adventurer Bear Grylls who, as a survival expert, would no doubt concur with BP's insistence on scouts having 'a state of readiness in mind and body' at all times.

Being prepared, trying to foresee eventualities, working out what might happen and then making plans to deal with it, is the bread-and-butter not only of military leaders but business people, party planners, scientists, musicians and many an aspiring domestic goddess

> "Be Prepared...' the meaning of the motto is that a scout must prepare himself by previous thinking out and practising how to act on any accident or emergency so that he is never taken by surprise."
>
> *Robert Baden-Powell, founder of the Scouting Movement*

too. Preparing and planning is something we all do to some extent every day. It's a task that requires imagination and practicality, and it depends on our own attitude towards time itself as to how we go about it in every day life.

What kind of future?

There are some of us for whom the future is much more attractive, safer, more energising in prospect, if it's planned. We are secure when we know there is a plan, when we know we've done all we can to make it work. We can see the way ahead and it looks organised.

There are others of us who much prefer the future when it is unknown. Plans make us feel hemmed in, anxious, claustrophobic. After all, who knows what might happen? Flexibility is key, the future is thrilling when we don't know what's going to happen and any attempt to nail us down is resisted!

These personality preferences reveal some of our attitudes towards time and for any of us who have attempted to work in teams, perhaps trying to organise an event, will know that these differences can cause tension if team members don't understand each other's perspective.

What are essentially strengths can be turned into negatives; when one person thinks they're being 'flexible and open' that can appear to others as 'disorganised'. On the other hand, one person's attempts to be 'clear and prepared' can make others feel hemmed in.

And we all know that the best-laid plans don't always work. In the military, the adage is that plans never survive contact with the enemy. We know too the old Yiddish proverb: 'When human beings make plans, God laughs'.

But in Advent, Scripture's wisdom about preparation and its place in our spiritual lives is given pride of place. Jesus told a number of stories about living in a state of readiness for the coming of the Lord. There were the ten women who thought ahead enough to buy oil for their lamps, trimming their wicks, as they waited during the night for the bridegroom to return. The other ten who didn't prepare ran out of light. (Matthew 25.) Jesus even went so far as to say that God's arrival in our lives, in the world, would be like the arrival of a thief in the night:

Keep awake therefore, for you do not know on what day your Lord is coming. But understand this: if the owner of the house had known in what part of the night the thief was coming, he would have stayed awake and would not have let his house be broken into. Therefore you also must be ready, for the Son of Man is coming at an unexpected hour. (Matthew 24.42-44.)

Jesus's stories combine a sense that we must at all times be prepared - but be prepared for surprises, for which we can't prepare.

Practising your courage

But what are the main elements of this state of readiness that Jesus urges? In his parables, quite often the main protagonist – the land-owner or the master of the house or the bridegroom – has gone away. There is a group of people who wait for the main actor to return and their attitude, Jesus teaches, is an attitude of readiness and preparedness. One of the key elements of preparation in the real world for real-time events is practice. Practising, and repeating the practice, for example, baking a trial cake way before the party to see whether it works, is an aspect of being ready - of getting ready.

The spiritual practice that Jesus describes - that of being prepared - also requires practice, but perhaps not quite in the same way. In the gospels, what we're being asked to be ready for is not so much a future event (like a party - although Jesus tells stories about these kinds of parties to help us understand) it's closer to the idea of living eternally in the present: ready, awake, open, in order to greet God, who paradoxically, is already here.

The practice that Jesus is urging us to learn is not so much making a plan for every eventuality in the future (as we do with a party or a test) but living each day as if it were the day itself.

This gives us a whole new agenda for living. We're asked to practise our courage, practise openness and honesty, practise kindness, practise forgiveness. And to do all of this today - not postpone it all to some time in the future. Practising our courage, for example, means that we will commit to being as brave as we can in the small things now, so that it has become a habit by the time we need it for the big things. This might mean practising saying what we really do think about something that doesn't matter - even if we're worried about a potential reaction - so that when it does matter, we have something like a reservoir of courage to draw on in order to speak our mind.

Facing the past

Another key element of spiritual practice in the present, in order to be prepared for the future, is our attitude towards the past. Past anxieties, griefs, regrets, past resentments can become what the poet William Blake called 'mind-forg'd manacles'. That is, shackles of our own making, which stop us practising courage in the present in order to prepare for God's future. These can be all kinds of shackles: something we wish we'd said, someone we wish we'd stood up to, some kind of meanness we exacted on someone else who really didn't deserve the sharp end of our temper. These shackles can also be assumptions that haunt us: that we're not really good enough, that we can't really do what we want to do, what life coaches call 'self-limiting beliefs'.

And these 'mind forg'd manacles' or 'self-limiting beliefs' have been made by our experience of life, so we also need to ask for God's guidance about what to do with our past. The past is resolutely unchangeable, and what we did in the past stays there forever. Although this is a very obvious thing to say, it is surprisingly hard to accept; we go over things in our minds, decisions we've taken, paths not taken. In order to open ourselves up in the present, we have to have a way of dealing with our past. How to do that? Jesus's teaching was that we learn to live in the knowledge of God's inexhaustible forgiveness.

> "Especially for those of us who lived in single cells, you had the time to sit down and think, and we discovered that sitting down just to think is one of the best ways of keeping yourself fresh and able, to be able to address the problems facing you, and you had the opportunity, also, of examining your past."
>
> *Nelson Mandela*

> "I always had a philosophy which I got from my father. He used to say, "Listen. God gave to you the gift to play football. This is your gift from God. If you take care of your health, if you are in good shape all the time, with your gift from God no one will stop you, but you must be prepared."
>
> *Pele, Brazilian footballer*

Anne Lammott puts it well in her book *Help Thanks Wow: the Three Essential Prayers:* 'there are three things I cannot change – the past, the truth and you.'

Rowan Williams makes the same point in *Lost Icons*: 'whatever is said, the past remains violently, itself, a foreign country indeed.'

And a much quoted truism, said to have been said not least by one condemned prisoner facing execution is that 'to forgive is to give up all hope of a better past'.

These are hard truths to accept. But Jesus's teaching acknowledges that it's hard, by insisting on praying for forgiveness ourselves and praying for a forgiving heart towards other people. It's right in the middle of the Lord's Prayer, a key and fundamental part of his teaching. Practising forgiveness in the present begins

> "I wander thro' each charter'd street,
> Near where the charter'd Thames does flow.
> And mark in every face I meet
> Marks of weakness, marks of woe.
>
> In every cry of every Man,
> In every Infants cry of fear,
> In every voice: in every ban,
> The mind-forg'd manacles I hear."
>
> *from William Blake's poem: 'London'*

to redeem an unchanging past and prepares us for God's renewed presence in the future.

It's a distinctive aspect of Jesus's teaching that we should prepare for the coming of the kingdom in the ways we've been exploring. But there is an aspect of preparation that can be dangerous for us.

The snare of preparation

Russian novelist Leo Tolstoy wrote about, 'the snare of preparation'. His point was a generational one, arguing that at the very moment when young people have huge energy and ideas to change the world, civilised societies ensnare them in a system of education that renders them inactive; learning, preparing.

Tolstoy's point about society and its organisation of education is controversial and I don't propose to explore it in depth here, but his idea of a potential *snare of preparation* is one that can resonate with us in everyday life too. The opposite of the Nike slogan 'Just do it', we can ourselves be ensnared in a state of mind that permanently tells us we're not ready; we're waiting until we've had more experience, have practised one more time, we're waiting until we've had a bit more training, waiting until we've had one more meeting. Sometimes preparation can be a cover for the fact that we're actually afraid to act. And so we keep putting it off, telling ourselves we're laying the groundwork, working ourselves up to it, waiting for the right moment. Which sometimes never comes.

In the gospel stories about the weeks leading up to Jesus's arrest, trial and execution, you get the sense that after he has set his face towards Jerusalem, Jesus is acting while he waits for others to choose the precise moment of his betrayal. He doesn't hand himself in, and so he is not in control of the timing of events, although he almost goads the soldiers who arrest him at night, reminding them that he'd been available and visible in the Temple for a while before that. His own state of readiness is acute but even he is at the mercy of others with regard to timing.

Feeling prepared

The reality is that we will almost certainly never feel prepared for the reality of God's renewed presence in our lives and, in line with Jesus's teaching, our task is not to predict the future or to try to assess it, but to live now as if it were then. To live now, rooted in the hope of a new future, the coming of the *basilea*, the kingdom of God, that Jesus spent so much time talking about, where the hungry are fed and the captives are free.

This kind of preparedness is described well by the American theologian Walter Wink who gave a great definition of hope. He wrote that 'hope imagines the future, and then acts as if that future is irresistible'. This gives us an agenda for living in the real world while looking in hope for signs of a better one. And so our daily life can be transformed. We are not afraid that God's arrival is like a thief in the night; we're not made anxious by the plans that we know probably won't quite work as we want them to. Listening to the stories of Jesus of the men and women who waited and lived in a state of hope and readiness means that we more easily notice the everyday miracles with which life is saturated.

And this is a way of life that can be lived in any context at any time. Our models must surely be two of the older people in the gospels, who could be

"Master, now you are dismissing your servant in peace,
according to your word;
for my eyes have seen your salvation,
which you have prepared in the presence of all peoples,
a light for revelation to the Gentiles
and for glory to your people Israel."

Simeon's song Luke 2.29-32

forgiven for winding down, but who seemingly went about their everyday business attentive to the astonishing truth that God was with them in a new way. Simeon and Anna.

At the beginning of February each year the Church calendar kind of rocks on its axis. After all the excitement of Advent and Christmas, then the lovely season of Epiphany in January when we hear about all the revelations of God in the world, we arrive at 2nd February. This is called the feast of Candlemas or the Presentation of Christ in the Temple. And in the Church's year, it's the turning point. We turn from Christmas and all the joy of Christ's birth to focus our attention on Holy Week, recalling his death.

In the story told in Luke's gospel, Joseph and Mary take Jesus, as they are expected to do, to the Temple. The old priest Simeon sees the baby and realises that his life of waiting is over. His prayer is immediate: *'Lord now lettest thou thy servant depart in peace, for mine eyes have seen thy salvation.'* (Luke 2.29-30.) Anna the prophet, aged 84, similarly recognises Jesus and rejoices with the perhaps slightly bemused parents.

For us, it is a fruitful spiritual exercise to ask ourselves, 'What has to happen in my life, or in the world, for me to be able to say, with Simeon, if I die today, it will be okay?' Sometimes this question can unearth buried desires or worries or things unresolved in our hearts. It can give us a sense of how to resolve them. We can also, by asking ourselves this question, learn to live more peacefully with those things that are unresolved, unmended, undone.

A state of preparedness

We are people of the Way; we walk the path of discipleship, talking as we go. And we're asked to live in a state of preparedness that means acting in the present to help bring a better future into being. One South American liberation theologian puts it well: we read Scripture with our feet as well as our eyes and our brains. That means we will always ask, as with the story about Simeon and Anna, how does this affect my life as I am actually living it?

Being prepared means practising and repeating the practice of being open, attentive. We learn that having this attitude is only deepened by taking action, often in small ways, everyday ways, to deepen our own commitment to a new future in God. In order to be free to do this, we have to take a look at our past, knowing that while we can't change it, we are able to reach out for the forgiveness that is already ours. And to know that our preparedness will ultimately make us hopeful and set us free.

Questions for Groups

1. 'Being dependent on God involves planning' says Lucy on track 25. Do you agree? Do you prefer the future when it's planned or when it's unknown?

2. Just as we all have different ways of imagining the future, we all deal with the past differently. So is it true, as Anne Lamott writes, that 'there are three things I cannot change – the past, the truth and you.'? *See p.18.*

3. Do you think Lucy's suggestions in her new agenda for living are realistic? See 'Practising your courage' on *p.16.*

4. Do you recognise the 'snare of preparation' - putting things off until you're a bit more ready? *See p.18 and track 26.*

5. Re-read the 3rd paragraph on p.16. Jesus's stories about people being rewarded for being prepared are striking – how do you react to them?

6. The story about Simeon and Anna raises profound questions for us: could you say, as Simeon did, that if you were to die today, all would be well? If your answer is no, what might you do about that before it's too late? *See p.20.*

7. 'Anna is patient but not passive' says Lucy on track 27. Anna's senses have been sharpened. Does old age inevitably bring patience? And wisdom?

8. Do you think the South American theologian who said that we read the Bible not only with our eyes but with our feet went far enough? What about with our heart and our head too, as Lucy suggests? *See p.20 and track 29.*

"You tell me: Can you live crushed under the weight of the present? Without a memory of the past and without the desire to look ahead to the future by building something, a future, a family? Can you go on like this? This, to me, is the most urgent problem that the Church is facing."

Pope Francis

Kairos and Chronos: is time running out?

Read: Revelation 22.1-13

I was walking my dog in the park recently, and a man was shrieking at a runner he was coaching, 'We need an extra ten seconds!' I couldn't help thinking – well, you can't have them! We've all got the same number of seconds and running faster won't get you any more. The runner, moving as fast as he could to gain the ten seconds, reminded me of an analogy I have found very helpful when thinking about the time that I have; that modern life is lived at such a pace that it is like trying to tell the time by looking at the second hand on a clock; it's accurate, but a rather breathless and hyperactive way to go about things. At its best, a life lived in synchronicity with the rhythms of God will be a life lived, not by the second hand, but by the hour hand: just as accurate, just as capable of identifying what is 'now', but lived with a different underlying rhythm and pace. Yet it still arrives at the same destination at the same time.

Who wants to live forever?

In the previous sessions we've been considering different aspects of life and reflecting on them in the light of Christian theological interpretations of time. The fundamental paradox though is that when we consider the purposes and presence of God, we are dealing with eternity, but when we think about ourselves, we are dealing with time. Imagining God existing beyond time is almost too difficult for us, yet it is the only thing that stops us from reducing God to terms we can manage. God can't be a thing that is outside us, a thing that we choose not to believe in. If God is God, then God simply is; like the air that we breathe.

C S Lewis captures something of the 'givenness' of God's presence when he comments that: 'I believe in Christianity as I believe the sun has risen. Not because I see it, but because by it I see everything else'.

The gospels are full of references to eternity and eternal life; living forever. I have had people say to me in pastoral situations that eternal life isn't really something they want although they think they should want it. Or as Freddie Mercury sang rather defiantly in 1986: 'Who wants to live forever?'

Christianity puts quite a lot of emphasis on living in eternity.

> "There is nowhere where God isn't."
>
> *Archbishop Rowan Williams*

> "O God, our help in ages past,
> our hope for years to come,
> our shelter from the stormy blast,
> and our eternal home.
>
> A thousand ages in thy sight
> are like an evening gone,
> short as the watch that ends the night
> before the rising sun."
> *from Isaac Watts' hymn*

And it's easy, when remembering all the references to eternal life in the gospels, to think that it somehow starts after we die. What is sometimes referred to as 'pie in the sky when you die'. But actually, if eternity is what it says it is, then it's already happening. Eternal life doesn't just start - it's eternal. So it's already happening now, here. And although we live our lives going about our everyday business, living by the watch on our wrist or the clock on our mobile, actually we are also living in what might be called God's time. Eternity.

Chronos meets *Kairos*

This can be mind-bending stuff. Philosophers have spent centuries trying to explain time and our attitude towards it. But I find it easier to think of characters and pictures rather than concepts and ideas. The Greeks expressed it like this when they developed their ideas about two kinds of time that we discern in our lives; one they called *chronos* – measurable time – and the other they called *kairos* – which has the sense of a 'right time'; a ripe,

fulfilled time. When the Greeks built statues to illustrate these ideas, they showed *Chronos* as a rather broken down figure, Old Father Time, quite wrecked by the relentlessly passing hours, tired out, exhausted by all the minutes he had lived through and sentenced to hold up the sky. *Kairos* on the other hand was drawn or sculpted as a young man, fleet of foot, elusive and free; a way of seeing time that is open ended and not strictly measured. *Chronos* seems earthbound, *kairos* is free to fly; *chronos* is measured in seconds, *kairos* is measured in moments.

Christian thinkers took up this distinction between *chronos* and *kairos*. In his second letter to the Corinthians, St Paul used it to talk about a favourable time, a 'now' kind of time which was the 'day of salvation'. Christian theology has developed this 'now' kind of time as a way of talking about eternal life lived now. We live immersed in life eternal while also living within time. This awareness of 'kairos', God's time, comes as a kind of 'eternal now'.

With these two characters, we can't help thinking that somehow 'kairos' is better than 'chronos'. *Chronos* makes us feel exhausted, running to keep up, maybe even a bit confining. *Kairos* on the other hand is more joyful, more awake, less broken down by it all, more energetic. In spiritual terms that may well be true, but it's important when we're trying to hold these two ways of thinking about time together that we're not too down on poor old *chronos.*

Being able to measure time accurately has enabled humanity to do immense good; to know how long a person can tolerate an anaesthetic for a life-saving operation, for example; or how long a person can safely dive to great depths to explore the wonders of the ocean. The measurable *'chronos'* time isn't bad; it's just not the whole truth.

And so, as ever, Christians are trying to hold two things together in faith: a sense that we live in time but we also live in the promise of an eternal now.

I also want to go further than that and say that separating these two ways of seeing time is actually dangerous. There are plenty of instances where a too-vivid belief in eternity has blinded us to human suffering in time. During the Reformation, heretics on all sides were burned to death in this life, supposedly to save them from the eternal fires of hell. Believing in an eternity that somehow starts in the future, with access to it depending on our behaviour in the present, leads to a twisted logic that can encourage the most vicious of condemnations, the cruellest of verdicts and the most brutal of punishments.

But if we accept that eternity is now, if we can understand both *chronos* and *kairos* as valuable and interdependent, then we take seriously people's immediate needs. We do not ignore their suffering in the name of an eternity that will arrive later and make it better. As the Christian Aid slogan goes: *We believe in life before death.*

Kairos becomes then, not a way of escaping real life, but a way of deepening and transforming our experience of life lived today; as well as giving us a hint of a deeper life lived for ever. And we deepen our sense of living in God's time by making chronological time for prayer.

So we're asked to live holding these two times together.

Imagining God's new future

When he shared the bread and wine at the Last Supper, Jesus said, 'Do this in remembrance of me'. But our sharing of Communion, however often we do it and whatever our church tradition, can't simply be a memorial service re-enacting something that happened in the past. Christianity is a religion fundamentally orientated towards the future; and our vision of the future is expressed when we share bread

"The western world has done away with religion but not with our religious impulses; we seem to need some higher purpose, some point to our lives - money and leisure, social progress, are just not enough."

Jeanette Winterson, author

and wine together. God's future is described often by Jesus as a banquet where the poorest, who have been brought in from the highways and byways, find a place. It is a banquet where all are fed and no one is left thirsty; a place where the last shall be first and the first shall be last.

Christianity teaches that human beings live in the gap between 'now' and 'not yet'. We live in the world as it is, as we are, full of injustices and hurts and ambiguities. But we also hope for more, for better. We know that even in the contradictory events and feelings that make up our everyday lives, there are hints of the possibility of resolution. A place where, to quote the Christian mystic Mother Julian of Norwich, 'All shall be well, and all shall be well and all manner of thing shall be well.'

One of the stories about Jesus in the gospels gets to the heart of this. He visits a pool that's said to have healing powers at a place called Bethesda. There he comes across a man who has been there for 38 years, trying to get himself into the pool to benefit from the healing waters. We never really learn what his difficulties are, but as he explains to Jesus, he's been stuck in these repetitive and futile attempts to change his own fortunes. In reply to Jesus's question:

'Do you want to be made well?' he doesn't really answer him but blames God; blames other people for getting in the way or for not helping him.

And so he is stuck, year after year, in a pattern of life that's wasting him away. In healing him, Jesus disrupts this pattern, jolts him out of his stuck-ness. In other words, Jesus's intervention breaks the pattern of *chronos* with *kairos*. The man is free from his repetitive pattern of life and the true meaning of Sabbath, the time in which this healing takes place, is revealed.

Strangely still

A final thought about these two ways of interpreting time. Moving from life in time to life in eternity is marked by the process we call death.

And this is the ultimate meditation on the meaning of time.

Most of us don't want to deal with this head-on. We avoid thinking about our own death. Because we live in chronological time, we can't imagine living in *kairos* time, although we may get intimations of it in meditation, on the top of a cliff on a beautiful day or looking at the night sky.

The transition from life in time to life in eternity, dealing with the prospect

> "Death is the end of a long school of letting go that has lasted a lifetime. It is learning from Christ, and an awareness that even in the midst of death we are called into life"
>
> *Fr Michael Paul Gallagher SJ*

of our own death, has been likened to a colossal leap of imagination necessary at the other end of life: our birth. If I try to imagine myself before I was physically born, I might not really be sure that my consciousness was capable of imagining life outside the womb.

There I am, in my mother's womb, living in fluid, safe in my own existence. I might be able to hear intimations of another life, voices or music, but I can't possibly imagine what it might be like to live in a different element, air - to be able to stand or run or shout. All these things are unimaginable to me, free floating as I am.

Moving on

But actually, in order to move to the next stage of life, I am about to embark on a perilous journey. I will suddenly, and without warning, learn to breathe. I will stop floating and start walking. We will change into a creature almost beyond recognition. It is a transfiguring experience and we will never, ever return to the life we knew.

Perhaps there is a spiritual parallel here. We live now in our bodies, whatever they're like, however they've developed, and it's all we know.

What we know about the passage of time we observe through our bodies. We can see that our bodies change over time, and they tell us that we are to expect death. It is a monumental effort of imagination to wonder what happens next. From a viewpoint of Christian faith, we are about to embark on a perilous journey not unlike the one we made when we were born. We are dying and simultaneously being born into what we might call the third stage of our life; we lived inside the womb, we lived on earth and now we will live in heaven.

For those of us who have not yet died, death remains stubbornly a mystery that we can't solve. In the words of the sociologist Dorothy Rowe, all that we know this side of death is that a person becomes 'strangely still'. Anything else is speculation.

Some spiritual writing talks about 'thin' places: places where heaven seems close to earth, where we become acutely aware that the passage between one and the other is no more than a heartbeat. These can be moments in time when we are aware of eternity now. We talk sometimes of time standing still. It can be at momentous moments - sitting with someone you love as they die. Or at moments that seem inconsequential - the way that sunlight catches a building, or an unexpected kindness.

I currently serve in the church where the poet William Blake was baptised. And his words accompany me as I go about my daily work because they are a beautiful way of expressing the paradox I've been trying to talk about in this session.

To see a World in a Grain of Sand
And a Heaven in a Wild Flower
Hold Infinity in the palm of your hand
And Eternity in an hour

Recognising eternity, even while we attempt to contain it in an hour, gives us a clue of what lies beyond the stillness of our bodies and the silencing of our voice. And we might be able to imagine saying, in answer to Freddie Mercury's question: 'Who wants to live forever?' Well, I think I do.

> "I have always been delighted at the prospect of a new day, a fresh try, one more start, with perhaps a bit of magic waiting somewhere behind the morning."
>
> *J B Priestley, writer and social commentator*

Questions for Groups

1. Tell a story of when, for you, you felt time slowed right down or perhaps stood still. Can you talk about what prompted this sense and why?

2. Lucy has met people who were unsure whether they really wanted eternal life, even though they thought they probably should want it. Do you think there is a difference between 'eternal life' and 'living for ever'? *See p.22. and track 33 of the audio/transcript.*

3. What do you think of Lucy's distinction between *chronos* time and *kairos* time? Do you recognise it or not? *See p.23 and track 32 of the audio/transcript.*

4. The man at the pool at Bethesda was asked by Jesus, 'Do you want to be well?' This is a profound question for all of us. What's your answer to this question? What might 'well' look like for you in your life?

5. *Listen to track 35.* Do any of the experiences described resonate with you?

6. Many, perhaps most, of us are afraid of dying. Some people aren't. What's your feeling? What, for you, would be 'a good death'?

7. Do you find the parallel that Lucy draws between birth and death helpful? *See p.26.*

8. On tracks 37 and 38 'thin places' are discussed. Where do you stand on this? Have you experienced something like a 'thin' place where it seemed that the eternal God was very close? *See also p.26.*

RECEIVING CHRIST

'To all who received him ... he gave power to become children of God.' (John 1.12.) This raises big questions. Aren't we all children of God anyway? What does it mean to have 'a relationship with God'? This course teases out from the NT various ways in which we receive Christ. St John's theology in his magisterial Gospel has practical implications for our day-to-day lives.

With Bishop Nick Baines, Margaret Sentamu, Revd Dr Ken Howcroft and Theodora Hawksley

THE PSALMS

Course booklet written by Bishop Stephen Cottrell

These ancient poems have stood the test of time for they address many of the problems we still face: violence, injustice, anger – and bewilderment. This course reflects on the psalms in general (and five psalms in particular).

With Fr Timothy Radcliffe, Revd Preb Rose Hudson-Wilkin, Revd John Bell and Revd Dr Jane Leach

PRAISE HIM
songs of praise in the New Testament

Course booklet by Dr Paula Gooder

This course explores five different Songs of Praise from the New Testament – what they tell us about God and Jesus, but also reflecting on what they tell us about ourselves and our faith.

With Archbishop Justin Welby, Sr Wendy Beckett, David Suchet CBE and Moira Sleight.

BUILD ON THE ROCK
Faith, doubt – and Jesus

Is it wrong – or normal and healthy – for a Christian to have doubts? Is there any evidence for a God who loves us? We hear from many witnesses. At the heart of a Christian answer stands Jesus himself. We reflect upon his teaching, death, resurrection and continuing significance.

With Bishop Richard Chartres, Dr Paula Gooder, Revd Joel Edwards and Revd David Gamble.

GLIMPSES OF GOD
Hope for today's world

Course booklet by Canon David Winter

We live in turbulent times. This course draws on the Bible, showing where we can find strength and encouragement as we live through the 21st century.

With Rt Hon Shirley Williams, Bishop Stephen Cottrell, Revd Professor David Wilkinson and Revd Lucy Winkett.

HANDING ON THE TORCH
Sacred words for a secular world

Worldwide Christianity continues to grow while in the West it struggles to grow and – perhaps – even to survive. What might this mean for individual Christians, churches and Western culture, in a world where alternative beliefs are increasingly on offer?

With Archbishop Sentamu, Clifford Longley, Rachel Lampard and Bishop Graham Cray.

RICH INHERITANCE
Jesus' legacy of love

Course booklet by Bp Stephen Cottrell

Jesus left no written instructions. By most worldly estimates his ministry was a failure. Yet his message of reconciliation with God lives on. With this good news his disciples changed the world. What else did Jesus leave behind – what is his 'legacy of love'?

With Archbishop Vincent Nichols, Paula Gooder, Jim Wallis and Inderjit Bhogal.

WHEN I SURVEY...
Christ's cross and ours

Course booklet by Revd Dr John Pridmore

The death of Christ is a dominant and dramatic theme in the New Testament. The death of Jesus is not the end of a track – it's the gateway into life.

With General Sir Richard Dannatt, John Bell, Christina Baxter and Colin Morris.

"the York Course sets the standard for Lent courses ... it always opens up discussion." **Church Times** reviewer